Nine Seeds to Sow for Personal Growth

A guide for directing your life with intention.

Dwayne J. Lattimore

WEconomy/ ATTN: Dwayne J. Lattimore
2472 Jett-Ferry Rd. Ste 400-127
Dunwoody, Georgia 30338

First edition published May 2021

Cover Art by Dwayne J. Lattimore

All production designs are trademarks.
For information regarding bulk purchases of this book, digital purchase and special discounts, please contact the author.

Visit our website at www.thinkweconomy.com

ISBN: 978-0-578-90845-8

The opinions expressed in the book are for general informational purposes only and are not intended to provide financial advice or recommendations. It is strongly advised to seek professional counsel before making any financial decisions.

Table of Contents

Your mind is a garden. Plant and each seed carefully.

-Dwayne J. Lattimore

Acknowledgments

God,
Thank you for empowering me when I felt there was no hope. I'm not a perfect man, and your mercy is second to none. Thank you for forgiving me for anything foolish I had ever done and seeing the good in me when I didn't deserve it. Please use me through this book to be the voice of inspiration in someone else's life. With deep love. Thank you.

Dad,
I miss you terribly and wish that you were here to witness the great things I'm working on. I've always tried emulating your toughness to never back down and your brilliant intelligence. Time will never fade your legacy. I think of you daily twenty-plus years later. You were and still are my hero. I promise that your grandchildren will know what a great man you were. I love you dearly. I hope I've made you proud.

Mom,
Thank you for being the pillar of strength when I didn't know if I would live or die as a child. You stood firm where many parents would've become broken both physically and emotionally. The word resilience should have your picture next to it in the dictionary. You've worked very hard to provide a good life for me and my sister, and I pray that my success will one day be able to make sure you'll never want for anything. I love you.

To my Sister,
I never knew that you would be so supportive of me in our adult years. Many siblings in various families don't have close relationships after they move away from home. You've been the voice of strength and reason in countless situations. I can't begin to express in words how lucky I am to have a big sister like you. Your words of wisdom and spirituality continuously ground me. You're one of the only people in this world I can honestly say that I trust wholeheartedly. Thank you Nyiesha. I love you.

To My Children,
God's greatest gift to me was becoming a father. You both have taught me patience and have given me the drive to try my hardest even when my motivation is dry. Your births have caused me to make positive changes to become the best version of myself. My life is meaningless without the love the two of you give so generously. Daddy will make you both proud. I promise.

Grandmaw & Grandpaw,
You two were a significant influence on my life. It hurts that neither of you ever had the opportunity to meet your great-grandchildren. Grandmaw, thank you for inspiring me to be a boss and giving me words of encouragement growing up. You're still the best cook I've ever known in my life. Grandpaw, I want to thank you for always making me think deeper about life and always challenging me to do more with my mind. You're the one who also taught me the skills I needed to be a great visual artist. Thank you for being a father figure in my life when my dad passed away. I'll never forget our conversations over coffee in the morning or the late-night rides across the bridge to Kentucky. Thank you both for giving me great memories that I'll hold on to forever. I love you both.

Special Thanks:
Michael Speller- Thanks for always being the big brother I never had. Rest well.

Thank you to all of my supporters who believe in "our" mission! Becoming a better person through growth, experience, spirituality, and our service to others is our purpose! May all your dreams become a reality and inspire those around you!

Foreword

Your mind is a garden. The title of this book gives strong emphasis on seeds. All seeds must be planted in the correct soil and given adequate water and nutrients before one day sprouting into a beautiful plant. Each idea we allow into our minds is like adding seeds to our mental soil. Sometimes, we may accidentally plant weeds by making incorrect decisions, which may compromise our garden's growth. These are commonly bad relationships with friends, family, lovers, addictions, horrible spending habits, and more. Each chapter's intention in Nine Seeds to Sow for Personal Growth is about instilling a tiny seed of an idea into your mind. It will be your responsibility to nourish and develop what's in your garden so that you may yield a wealth of personal growth!

Before you begin your journey through this book, there are a few seeds I'd like to plant in your mind before the rain comes. There aren't any wrong or correct answers to these questions simply because we all have unique life experiences. Why did you purchase this book? What do you hope to gain from reading this literature? Most importantly, what defines your purpose? Personal change isn't always as easy as putting on clean undergarments or shaving unwanted hair off your body. It can tax you emotionally and physically. It can build and dismantle personal relationships with associates, friends, and family. When you decide to embark on a new path by adopting new ways of thinking, you're guaranteed to experience many unforeseen challenges. Your purpose will carry you through the rough moments when your ship finds itself beaten by waves of opposition.

My daughter Egypt and my son Amir give me purpose. My little girl is the oldest; I can remember the day she was born, my priorities in life became more severe to me than ever before. I had always been about my business, but her birth kicked me in sixth gear. There were days I barely had food in the refrigerator, and once I became a father and had to answer to the dependency of my beautiful children, no food in the fridge was no longer acceptable. My efforts had to increase because I no longer lived an independent lifestyle. We often believe that we're performing at our highest level until met with the unknown, which gives us the "wake-up call" and the ability to summon a will so powerful that we become amazed at ourselves. You may find yourself in the mirror asking, "Who is this person?" That person is you! That "person" is the fearless version of you. Wouldn't it be nice to unleash this individual permanently?

There's immeasurable power in purpose. When your money isn't sufficient, it will carry you. When someone tells you that your dream is impossible, it'll prove critics wrong. It doesn't matter what your purpose is if it means the world to you! That's why I said earlier that there's no wrong or correct answer to the preceding questions because we're all different as human beings and must have mutual respect for one another's goals and intentions. What fuels my drive may not spark the slightest motivation in another individual. No matter how silly, bizarre, boring, glamorous, extreme, or impossible your goals may appear to others, guard and protect them with clarity.

On some occasions, depending on who you're talking to, it may be a good idea to keep these things to yourself. We all know negative people who are anxious to cut down someone else's ambitions. As if you don't already have enough to deal with daily, who wants that negative energy? The only people you should lend your ear to are those who offer constructive criticism and encouragement. Seek these people out and keep them around you. Develop a positive support system early in your journey. You'll need it, and you deserve it! Stay on your path and let your purpose motivate you through challenges.

If you have no intentions of acting on this book's principles, it's futile to continue reading. Personal change is like a physical workout requiring you to burn calories by thinking and doing! We're human, and we all may experience moments where we become unsure of ourselves or begin to lose the fire we once had when we started our journeys. You shouldn't feel bad about it. It's prevalent. However, it would be best if you remain resilient. Just as Coca-Cola brands itself regularly in restaurants on drinking cups and even unrelated things like sports complexes, you need to advertise your purpose to yourself daily! Get creative on how you'll do this. It doesn't have to be as expensive as a Coke ad, but perhaps writing it on a piece of paper and putting it inside the front door of your home as a reminder every time you exit.

My children's pictures are everywhere. I'm always running out of storage on my phone. I have too many videos and pics of them! However, they're the ones who give me purpose to bring the fight to an unforgiving world that could care less whether I make it or not. You are in control. You can change if you "will it" to happen. Thank you in advance for allowing me to share my experiences and personal views on life with you. Remember, these are just my ideas. Think of me as the friend who "gives it to you straight." This book isn't going to be a four-hundred-page marathon because I believe some things in life are cut and dry and do not warrant a drawn-out explanation. Why waste thirty minutes explaining something that can be achieved in less time? I value the time you're giving to me, and I don't want to abuse it with filler content—some ideas you may want to hear and others you may not. Real friends don't just tell you what you want to hear. They do their best to provide the truth! I'm not sure who said it first, but we've all heard it before, and that's that "The truth can hurt!"

Remember to be truthful with yourself while reading this book. Lying to yourself about your situation will not facilitate change. You're an extraordinary individual with unique abilities. I'm here to help you go deeper and improve upon who you already are. I hope that we can meet someday so that I may learn something from you. I wish you all the best and great fortune!

The First Seed
Reflection

We will begin this book starting with your worst enemy, the one on the other side of the mirror.

We all play a grave role in our self-destruction. We are our worst doubters, self-administer our worst criticisms, and nourish our bad habits. One of the significant weaknesses individuals in the world today have embraced is the habit of being too people-dependent. Let us not confuse this with the idea of interdependency, which has a purpose when two or more people/groups have a mutual dependence. An example of this would be airplane pilots and air traffic control personnel. We also aren't referencing those who should be people-dependent such as infants or humans with unfortunate disabilities. We are talking about those who limit themselves on accomplishing personal goals that solely rest upon having someone to do it with. If one of the partners suddenly decides that they don't want to do whatever the pair decided to do together, the whole operation falls apart. You'll often see this scenario play itself out many times over when countless people choose to have a "workout buddy" for visits to the fitness center. Do you know anyone like this? Have you been guilty of this yourself? Does this mentality say that you're dedicated to being physically fit? Why not go to the gym alone? Why do people constantly need the comfort of the company to give them the drive to achieve goals?

I've been guilty of everything mentioned above. I try my best to live without regrets, but I'm only human, and one major regret that I have is not exploring the world sooner.

8

I'm guilty of waiting to have a companion to travel overseas to visit places like Paris, France. I always felt that if I were going to enjoy a vacation, it had to be with a beautiful woman to experience it. Although this is still ideal in my mind, I realized that I'd cheated myself repeatedly waiting on a special someone. If I had the mindset that I have now, I would have many stamps on my passport. I allowed unique experiences to slip through my fingers because I was waiting on someone else to be present at the right time. The last straw was when I dated a woman for over a year and purchased a passport for her, and we ironically ended the relationship a few months later! I vowed from that point on that I would never do myself such a disservice again. If you have things to conquer in life, begin your journey alone if you must and let others join you on the way.

One of the more unique forms of people-dependence comes in the disguise of love. The inner euphoric experience attached to having a connection with a companion can become addictive as a drug. As humans, we tend to go out of our way to do what makes us happy, even if we know it isn't authentic or genuine. How many times have you witnessed someone end a relationship only to be in another in a short period? These people surely don't give themselves enough time to heal, reflect, or learn a valuable lesson from experience. Some people aren't comfortable being alone and need to "feel" loved by someone to be secure within themselves. I've asked several women about their initial interaction when a man approaches them, and the majority agree that a confident man is much preferable to the one who behaves desperately. It's better to learn to be confident and happy by yourself first. People will notice these types of attributes in you and will become attracted to them.

Remember to not cheat yourself out of the "growth" from the wisdom you can attain from each relationship before moving on to the next one. Your dealings with other people will not only teach you lessons about them, but you will also learn things about yourself. Although it may not have anything to do with love, everyone remembers the endless marathon Tom Hanks ran in Forrest Gump. He started running alone but later found hordes of people running behind him because they were inspired and attracted to his mission! Confidence is beautiful! There is nothing wrong with being single while working on personal endeavors. Stand tall even when alone, and soon, you'll find yourself surrounded by those who admire your strength and fearlessness.

If anyone is to be successful in this world, he or she must know that there will be many times they'll be without a support system. No one will be there to coach you or cheer you on. Your safety net won't be there to catch you from falling. Sometimes hitting the ground is good for you. It builds strength and character. There will be many times where it seems the world is against you, and everyone you may have thought was in your corner isn't giving the encouragement you expected. I want you to ask yourself an honest question. Have you been guilty of being people-dependent? How many things have you put on hold waiting for others?

I would like you to challenge yourself to begin breaking this psychological illness by doing a few random things:

1. Go to a lovely restaurant where couples are known to patronize and have dinner alone. Write down your experiences as you interact with the staff. Most of them will surely ask you if you're waiting on someone else to join.

Also, write down how you honestly felt during the experience. Go home and reflect.

2. Make time to watch a movie alone on a Friday or Saturday evening when the theater has a large crowd. Don't go during the early matinee when no one notices you and only five people are viewing the screening. Make a note of your experience as you will with the restaurant.

There are many other challenges that I could give you, but these are very easy and affordable to do by most people. Not to mention, there are many other activities that most people refuse to do alone. The point of these exercises is to get you into the habit of being comfortable with yourself. It's okay to be alone at times. Being alone helps you to understand yourself a lot better when not being influenced by others. You're able to find out who you are and begin working on being a better version of yourself. When you learn to develop strength, ambition, and resilience from within, anything will become possible for you to accomplish. You should believe in your abilities by also having faith in God. It's not about going to church and being able to cry and sing with everyone there. It's how you behave in your actions that says a lot about what you believe.

Although I'm not religious, the Holy Bible taught me many great lessons. I remember the story about Peter. Jesus didn't ask Peter to step out of the boat and walk on water. He asked him to get out of a vessel that had other people in it so that he could do the impossible. This act required blind faith while leaving friends behind. No one else got out of the boat. Only Peter. He had to accomplish it alone. When will you step out of your boat? Are you willing to leave others behind who are holding you down in life? Can you break your self-doubt as Peter had to learn to do? Why block all of life's potential blessings waiting on everyone else to get out of the boat?

Before I wrap up this chapter, I don't want you to believe that I'm co-signing an "I don't need anyone in the world" bravado. No one in this world is entirely autonomous. You will always need other human beings for something in life, whether they're giving you free favors or making you pay for their services.

Ex. Your money won't grow legs and fly a jet to your favorite destination.

You will indirectly pay a pilot by purchasing airline tickets or timeshares. Therefore, you need that individual for his or her services. However, this doesn't mean that you become people-dependent. Cooperation and interdependence are the necessities of world functionality. They should not be confused with goal-hindering dependence which relies on the agendas of others to get motivated.

Seeds to Sow:

- Reflect daily on your actions. It would be best if you constantly re-evaluated yourself to correct anything that could keep you from reaching your full potential. An individual's goals can traverse many areas, whether in business, health, romance, education, or several other places.

- Happiness is a responsibility.

- It's always been easy to blame others for reasons why things aren't going our way in life. Be accountable when you reflect.

- What role are you playing in your regression or progression? Get out of your way and start living the life you deserve!

The 2nd Seed
Time Allocation

The greatest asset that you have in the world is your time. Once it's gone, it's gone forever. Once you're born into this world, the countdown to your exit begins. Humans do not have the gift of immortality. Hence, we must allocate this precious resource very carefully. Many times, it's not until we've reached our elderly years that we understand the fragility of life because our youth gives us a false sense of eternity. Vigor has caused many to put off today's goals in the belief that they'll have *time* to do things in the future.

On many occasions, you can observe people and see where they invest most of their time. An excellent example of this would be someone who's much more muscular and athletic than the average person. Unfortunately, most humans don't have the gift of flawless genetics that allows them to acquire a physically fit appearance without some type of exercise regime. Many bodybuilders spend countless hours at the gym and monitor their nutrition intake very carefully. Things like protein, calories, fat, water, and vitamin intake are all micro-managed daily to achieve rare results. Injuries can occur, and adjustments must be made for recovery. We see examples of this with professional athletes every time we turn on stations such as ESPN. What would happen if this person decided to spend less time training at the gym and more time eating fast food and playing video games? Chances are, he or she would begin to lose their athletic appearance but would become very good at the video game that they're playing. The solution to achieving desired results in life is made by prioritizing the time spent on what

14

we value most and committing a fraction of that time to engage in things of less importance.

When was the last time that you compiled a list of all things that are important to you? Starting from the top, I challenge you to list things of utmost importance, with the least important at the very bottom. Take a moment and be honest with yourself when making your list. After you've completed this list, give the percentage of time next to each item that you genuinely believe you spend on each activity. When you have completed this, the total should be equal to 100%. Carefully monitor the percentages next to each item. Does your list perfectly go from the most significant portion of time spent from top to bottom? Remember, the top of the list should be your main priorities which should consume most of your time. Be honest when creating your list by not being selective in your daily activities. Things such as social media binging and spending hours viewing reality TV shows are all fair game!

Once you've completed the exercise above, you'll understand where some of your time is being squandered. This exercise could potentially reveal why you may not have accomplished specific goals in your life. The silver lining in all of this is that you have the power to make the adjustments necessary to reroute your time to more meaningful activities. The first step is always doing a self-analysis to determine where your time and resources are going. In the words of Peter Drucker, *"If you can't measure it, you can't improve it."*

People tend to *make time* for things that are important to them. Usually, when you hear someone say, "I don't have time to do that" or "I don't have time for that," usually what they mean is "I don't have time because I haven't tried managing it!" This could also mean that this person simply doesn't want to make time for whatever the subject may be. I used to contract for a primary phone carrier. There were plenty of idle hours while traveling between cities, so I would use part of that time to enjoy music. Most of my time was spent listening to study material or an audiobook. On an eight-hour drive, you could potentially breeze through at least two audiobooks. Look for windows of opportunity throughout your day to maximize your productivity. What about the workplace? What are you usually doing during your lunch break? Could you multitask and listen to educational material while eating your food? Could you study recorded notes from a lecture? Sure, you could! It would be a good idea to begin consistently questioning yourself about your daily time management. Think about how you can start leveraging all the hours you have available with creativity.

Punctuality
Working at the worst job I ever had taught me the importance of being on time. We weren't allowed to arrive after 7 am. If we got there early, we were on time. If we got there on time, we were considered late. If we got there late, the manager would send us home without any product to sell.

These practices directly affected how employees managed their time at work and at home. Knowing that you could negatively impact your income by showing up late was something you'd own. What are the consequences if your staff arrives late? How does this affect your business? What loss in revenue does this equal to over a year? Next-Day Air services at UPS aren't possible without their employees adhering to work schedules. Asking for this service is like "going to the front of the line." You want things done as quickly as possible, and you're willing to pay a premium.

However, if your package arrives late, you may be reluctant to use their service again. I would assume that adhering to your schedule is of utmost importance to a business where punctuality is the lifeblood. Develop time management policies within your organization that you and your staff can commit to.

Seeds to Sow:
- Accomplish as much as you can in the shortest amount of time possible.
- Learn to allocate your time to the things you value most before investing too much in activities that will prove useless to you in the long run.
- Remember, your time is your most valuable asset. Once it's gone, there's absolutely nothing you can do to get it back.
- Put punctuality into practice.

The 3rd Seed
Dating & Marriage

A companion can either be a blessing or a hindrance. The chemistry between a man and woman can cause anyone to make long-term decisions that weren't well thought out. Some of the people we meet on our relationship journey are here to stay, while others will come and go. Let's talk about the significant other to who we're devoting a large portion of our time.

Some may argue that we shouldn't examine those we invite into our lives with a magnifying glass. Just have fun and let things happen, right? Wrong. Suppose you're serious about becoming a very successful person and reaching every goal in life. In that case, you must align everything in that same path, including your relationships. Stagnation is unacceptable. Many men and women have engaged in toxic relationships that took the "wind out of their sails." It would be beneficial to date someone who supports your dreams.

Let's take a deeper approach to this. The longer you date someone, the more influence he or she will have over your life, whether you want to believe it or not. People you don't know could say the most disrespectful thing to you and barely hurt your feelings. Someone much closer to you could say the same rude something to you months later and deliver a crushing blow to you emotionally. Do you see where this is going? Now imagine the same person becoming very positive and supportive of your dreams and what that could do to fuel your inspirations.

Your companion doesn't have to share the same interests as you. What your companion should have is the desire to ascend beyond their current situation. Most parents tell their teenagers to graduate from high school and go to college where they'll find a good husband/wife. Why were our parents/guardians giving us this advice? They were indirectly explaining everything in this chapter because they've had a firsthand experience of pairing two people heading in the same direction versus those who aren't. No parent would ever recommend that their young adult go to college to engage in toxic relationships and pair up with someone who doesn't have goals. Doing so would create a hindrance to the development of the seeds planted in your garden!

Too many great people subject themselves to bad relationships, which allows their partner to "jail" their dreams. Your wife/husband should support everything that you do. Considering the level of influence they have over your decisions, the last thing an ambitious person wants to hear is:

"Why would you want to do something like that?"
"You've got to be kidding me!"
"Isn't someone already doing that?"
"I wouldn't do that if I were you. I would do this instead."
"That's going to cost way too much to get started."
"You can't do that!"
"We don't have the money for that."
"I wouldn't do that if I were you!"

All the statements listed above have one thing in common. People tend to correlate their strengths and weaknesses to that of others around them. The act is known as "projecting." Negative statements like those mentioned above are simply reflections of the confidence most people see only in themselves.

I've never seen a marriage where someone in the relationship isn't doing what their heart desires and can admit that they're pleased. For us to have the ability to be a blessing in someone else's life, we must first reach a level of self-contentment, or we will live in the shadow of our partner's success.

I've met countless men and women who love their companions with all their heart but hate the fact that they feel less of a husband or wife because they can't provide a means on the same level as their partner. Toxic spouses, boyfriends, girlfriends, etc., enjoy keeping you beneath them on the success totem pole to ensure that they're maintaining control of the relationship. Does this sound familiar to you?

The "glass ceiling" isn't just used in the workplace; it's also used at home! Whether in the home or the job market, the reason this roadblock exists is so that insecure individuals can gain leverage by staying in power over others. Progression becomes completely idle because no matter how hard you work, you will not advance. The race is fixed, and everyone is playing the same game with a different set of laws. You don't need to marry a person who will put a glass ceiling on your success to boost their ego. Family should build on a great support system that encourages everyone to do better. We can't do much about siblings who compete for our parent's attention while growing up. However, when we become adults, it's important to come home to a companion who fosters a supportive environment.

On many occasions, you'll discover that several people are only interested in talking about themselves, their goals, their objectives, and success stories. There won't be much concern about yours. Anyone who labels themselves as your significant other should be giving parallel attention to what's important to you. Success has never been an autonomous effort. In other words, we all feed off one another for encouragement because the road to success isn't one quickly dealt with alone. There will be various challenges such as a feeling of defeat, discouragement, laziness, etc., that could surface from any direction.

Same as a world champion boxer, you'll need a team of support. These are the people who are always in your corner, giving you words of encouragement and love that will provide you with the stamina to "stay in the fight."

For the sake of privacy, I'm going to use fictional names to make my next point. There's a guy named James that lives in Cincinnati, Ohio. James is roughly 31 years of age and has always been a very ambitious fellow. James is the type of guy that started so many different businesses but has yet to become financially successful. Without quitting his day job, he still manages to push forward in seeing that he makes his dream of entrepreneurship a reality. I admire James for this. After nearly losing all his money on a vending machine business, he hasn't lost hope at all. From time to time, James and I would grab drinks and discuss things affecting our economy. On one occasion, he seemed to be depressed and didn't have the drive to keep striving. Immediately I knew that something was wrong because this was out of character for the person I had grown to know. When I asked him why he was giving up on his dreams, he said, "Well, my girlfriend thought we ought to save our money and move into a bigger home."

I responded quickly, saying, "This seems like a serious relationship. Is she a nice girl?"

"Wayne, this girl is a drop-dead gorgeous man! Anytime we step out in public, guys start with jealousy!" said James.

I reiterated, "No, James. Is she a nice girl? What about her character? What does she do for a living?"

"Yeah, she's cool. I met her at a club in the brewery district seven months ago. We never argue about anything, and she goes to school part-time. We always enjoy each other's company, and she's always at my place, so we might as well live together," said James.

Paying closer attention to the conversation instantly revealed what I needed to know without James having to go on and on for the rest of the evening about his new girlfriend. My buddy James has allowed his "vision" to become clouded by his new girlfriend's beauty. He can't think intelligently about his personal goals or desires because her beauty has steered him down a path that only she can navigate. She told James to save his money and get a larger home. What warranted this upgrade and lifestyle? James' girlfriend had no formal or self-taught education in creating cash flow. The girlfriend, we will call her Nina, works at a bar and has become content with her position income-wise. She hasn't had the education to realize what James is trying to do is much better than a regular 9 to 5 and can result in endless income depending on his motivation. This is a typical situation where only one partner in the relationship is familiar with the difference between a liability and an asset. In contrast, the other partner is clueless about financial management. Most people want to have larger homes, televisions, automobiles, etc. but they're all "wants" and not "needs."

I could've told James to reconsider going back to the drawing board and getting his business off the ground. Still, we both know who had the most influence in this situation. Let's face it; we're all suckers for love. Nina has effective tactics that I will never have. James would have to be mentally and emotionally strong enough to walk away from a relationship in a scenario such as this. Humans have the gift of forecasting a bad situation before it happens. We must begin to train ourselves to listen to "the voice of reason" coming from within.

Those who have successful businesses have faltered many times on the road to success. One success typically comes out of several failed attempts. Going out and doing something will give you the most incredible experience in the world rather than just sitting around talking about the "one day" you'll act. More on that later in the book. James eventually got over Nina's looks and decided to sever his ties. Had he stayed with a woman who wasn't going to support his dreams, he would have become stagnant. He didn't have to say much when we met for a drink that day, but I could tell that his whole demeanor and energy levels were way off. Life is too short to allow someone else to put out the fire in your dreams. When James finds a woman who will support his endeavors, he'll most likely marry her and achieve tremendous success at what he's already doing.

The romantic relationships that we choose can be related to sports. When teams are playing at home, they tend to win a lot more than if they were away. In basketball, winning a game at home can be almost too easy when everyone in the stadium is shouting your name and encouraging you to score more points. However, when you're away from home on foreign territory, the crowds bully you into making bad decisions and thus scoring less. Sports teams take their bands, cheerleaders, and mascots on the road to combat the negativity that all the players will face while away from home. The NBA and other professional sports organizations realize the importance of encouragement and building on the team's morale. They're familiar with the hostility and vulgar language that the opposing team's fans are going to use to dismantle every bit of hope left in the visiting team's body.

In the 2008 elections, I think we can all agree that First Lady Michelle Obama was a significant part of President Barack Obama's victory. People against Obama used every tactic to bring him down and discredit him for all his achievements and even his birthplace. Could you imagine the intensity of the doubt that would cross a person's mind after dealing with so much opposition? Michelle Obama must be an extraordinary wife to Barack. I can't imagine the endless conversations they probably had at night before going to bed. A man can only take so much of a public beating. A supportive family structure to return home to is paramount.

Many people are unaware that Michelle Obama was doing very well for herself before Barack became president. In their 2006 tax return, Michelle Obama made an excellent living pulling in $273,618, which was $116,536 more than her husband, Barack. I think it's safe to say that money was not an issue with these two. When Barack had decided to run for president, Michelle had to make a huge decision. She would no longer be the breadwinner and would have to take a *financial backseat* for her husband to manage and execute his road to the presidency. How's that for support? There was no guarantee that Barack would be the next president of the

United States, but his wife was willing to make that kind of sacrifice. I've never had the pleasure of meeting the President or our First Lady. Still, I'm sure they have volumes of knowledge to share in the subject of supporting your spouse. Michelle realized the greater good in their situation and became the first African-American First Lady of The United States of America. Since then, I'm sure endless doors of opportunity have opened for both Barack and Michelle.

You Can't Make Them Drink.
One of the most common complaints I hear from ambitious people in close relationships is that their companion doesn't want to do better. Some people have a problem with turning the "talk" into "doing." Relationships can be highly frustrating when the situation has changed, but the people involved are reluctant to change. Let's suppose you have a beautiful relationship that has been budding for the last four years. You and your mate have zero financial problems or insecurities, and all the bills are paid on time. This amount of time is enough to get many people set in their ways. All of a sudden, you and your companion are expecting a child. To maintain your current lifestyle, you will have to develop a plan that will bring in more income and possibly more space for the new baby. For most people, this is more than enough to get them motivated to earn more income and maybe create wealth.

Meanwhile, others might begin to complain about why they can't do this or that. Mature individuals would assume that if some people don't do it for themselves, they'll surely do it for their children. This is not true. Most people who don't have any hope in life to transcend above their current situation won't find it even during something so meaningful. You can't make them drink. They either want it, or they don't. Have you ever seen a parent that pours out an aroma of jealousy against their own child's achievements? This behavior is an example of non-ambitious people having children who have demonstrated qualities they wished they had growing up. Just as in the movies, people with no ambition are like zombies waiting to turn you into one of them. Choose healthy relationships when trying to become a significant achiever.

Be very adamant about not allowing your relationships to dig the hole that eventually buries your motivation. I don't have all the answers to the world's questions. Still, I am smart enough to know that a healthy relationship is non-existent if someone in that relationship isn't happy with themselves. With all the money that celebrities must waste at a moment's whim, one would assume that they have the most beautiful relationships on the planet. It's a standard miscalculation to think that money alone will solve most people's problems in relationships. Your goals may not include monetary gain but may need financial support to become a reality, such as building a school for children in underfunded neighborhoods. You could also be starting a movement against the social inequality for women in the corporate world. Whatever your intentions, you should always see your significant other cheering alongside you for the entire journey.

Seeds to Sow:
- Consider the role you have been playing in your relationships? Are you supportive?
- Is your attitude on the home court or with the visiting team? What about your companion?
- Does any of the above remind you of someone in your family, such as your mom or dad? What changes can you make to be a better partner?

- Have you ever discussed your personal and joint goals with your significant other? How can the two of you collaborate to make them a reality?

The Fourth Seed
Socially Engineered Success

Seed 4, Socially Engineered Success

Birds of A Feather

Proverbs 27:17 says, "Iron sharpeneth iron; So a man sharpeneth the countenance of his friend. Iron makes iron sharp, so a man makes sharp his friend. As iron sharpens iron, so friends sharpen each other's faces."- --The Holy Bible

Just as you've learned to choose the right companion. Friends can be a significant boost to your successful mindset or the opposite. Our mothers and fathers were very wise when they told us to be mindful of the company we keep. Birds of a feather really do flock together. One of the hardest things about some friendships is when you're the one who has the motivation, but one of your friends doesn't. We hate to see our comrades struggle and be unhappy, so we do our best to push them to strive for more. We should do this in moderation because it can appear that you're selfishly selling your vision to them. Many of us have long-term friendships that have lasted through the most challenging times, and watching a close friend walk away from their dreams can make the heart heavy. The reality is that time is slipping away each day. You can't afford to wait for others to want better for themselves. You must reduce the time you spend with peers who lack drive and allocate it towards those who aspire to do more with themselves.

28

In my early years of education, I went to school in downtown Cincinnati, Ohio. It was an art school full of students and teachers from every walk of life. Although the downtown area was mainly home to underprivileged families (apart from riverfront properties), my schooling environment was diverse. I made good friends that were deemed to be my friends forever, considering that this school started from the 4th grade and went all the way up to the 12th! That may sound weird, but it's very accurate! In fact, if you attended that school from the 4th grade to your senior year in high school, you were deemed a "survivor." I, however, was immediately disqualified from ever earning that title since I had begun attending in my 5th-grade year. You've probably heard of my childhood school before. It's called The School for Creative & Performing Arts, where I was an art major. This is where I met my former best friend during my 7th-grade year. We will call him Thomas.

Thomas and I didn't start off as friends. We kind of resented one another because we hadn't indeed known each other's character. The common denominator between Thomas and me was my cousin Ramiah with whom he shared an art class. We were all art majors. Thomas enjoyed hanging out with Ramiah, which eventually lead to us becoming good friends and later "best friends." Those were good times in my life. Ramiah, Thomas, and I cracked plenty of jokes to the point of overkill. We squandered no moment to tease one another as young boys do. During the next few years in school, Thomas and I did everything we could to attend the same classes so we'd always stay close. Best friends always seem to have a unique connection. I often would laugh on the inside about something while restraining myself from making too much noise. Thomas would know what I was laughing about without even having to ask!

Ramiah and I had the same weird, almost borderline telepathic connection.

As time went by, Thomas and I started a comic book series together, which we tried to have published. None of the publishing companies were taking us seriously at the time. However, it was still an excellent time for the memories it created. I penciled our drawings while Thomas was the designated inker. If my memory serves me correctly, it was mid-summer in the late 90s. One of Thomas's neighbors had been introduced to me, as he would be attending SCPA the next school year. We will call him Steve. We were picking up the pace of our comic book, and to my surprise, I found out that Steve was also an artistic individual with great skill. This was fantastic! I had two friends I began hanging out with heavily who happened to be in the arts just like me! The three of us had dreams of becoming big-time illustrators in hopes of gaining attention from companies like Marvel. Although that dream never materialized, we still had great moments together while enjoying the process. Our collaborative efforts in our teenage years were great practice in preparing us for the real world.

When I, Thomas, and Steve were sixteen years old, we used to go to the Mercedes-Benz dealership in Cincinnati, Ohio, to browse vehicles. These vehicles had a sticker price worth more than the homes we lived in. What was very impressive about the Mercedes dealership was that the salesmen knew we were young and aspiring to have nice cars. However, they still treated us as if we had the money in the bank to purchase their vehicles. We made several trips to the Mercedes dealership in the Kenwood area and a Land Rover dealership a little further down the street. My best friends and I had somewhat achieved these goals much later in life. While we all wanted Range Rovers, Thomas purchased a silver Land Rover, and Steve's mom bought him a new Chevy Impala. I had bought myself an all-white Infiniti QX56 (courtesy of the real estate company I later developed). We were very young walking into those dealerships and barely had enough money to keep gas in our vehicles at the time. I'm sure that one of the adults working at either one of these places knew a thing or two about vision. The salesmen at the dealerships were probably thinking, "Here goes a few fine young men with high standards." We believed in our dreams and always kept them in mind, putting our goals in front of us at the dealerships.

Ramiah and I used to draw large graphic pictures of ourselves stepping out of limos in front of our monstrous homes that we hoped to have someday. At the time, Ramiah and I didn't live in affluent communities, but we both knew where we wanted to be when we got older. The environment that swallowed up the dreams of so many children could never trap our minds where our physical bodies were. Keeping all things in mind, how could this affect the world that we currently live in? How can we as a people reach others who have fallen victim to their environmental circumstances? Coming from some of the worst situations myself, I can honestly say it was God, my family, and good social networking.

One good friend of mine is my barber. I believe all men and women could agree that going to the barber or beauty salon has more value than just the aesthetic services. My barber and I have become increasingly close because of the values we share in business. The ironic part about this is that our relationship wasn't like what we share now while in college. He was in a fraternity, and I was not. As we became men after college and began experiencing life, our values and goals had to transition with all that was transforming around us. We're both big fans of authors like Robert

31

Kiyosaki, Garrett Sutton, and many other great authors and public icons who've demonstrated their breadth of knowledge in business. Our conversations always included creative ways to advertise our businesses, exciting motivational books, and more. We rarely felt discouraged about our goals. Whenever we departed, we both left feeling energized by the other person's ambition. Our interaction was an example of iron sharpening iron.

Dealing with Jealousy, Envy, & Resentment
I'm a firm believer that not everyone was meant to be a permanent part of your life. Progression will sometimes mean cutting off dead weight, even if that means friends and relatives. A ship can't sail while being anchored at the port. Real friends will celebrate your victories because they know that a win for you is a win for the whole team! This doesn't mean that if your colleague becomes wealthy, they should become your private lending institution. This indicates that you have the opportunity to learn and be influenced! When your moment comes, you will reciprocate these same qualities.

As children, many of us grow up through adolescence with hopes of becoming highly successful individuals. While some may take longer than others, at the end of the day, what matters is if you've reached your full potential or not. Some may argue that their friends love to boast about their accomplishments and label them conceited. While there are countless self-absorbed people on this earth, I don't believe that everyone who gives testimony about their success deserves criticism. It's easy to make an opinion about the person you see in the present when you can't identify with their past. What about those individuals who understand the struggles you've endured but yet, still envy you? This is a form of jealousy that causes family, friends, or associates to become discreetly resentful when your progress reminds them of their shortcomings.

Those who identify with me personally know that my journey was very challenging growing up. My family never lived in the best neighborhoods. I never had the best health, and every temptation or obstacle that could be thrown into my path had been placed. Therefore, I would find it very disheartening knowing someone close to me felt a sense of jealousy. However, this does not disregard the possibility of it occurring. Those relationships can become cancerous and potentially damage other healthy connections in your circle. Remember to ask yourself what having a relationship with someone is costing you.

Social Engineering
I never had the desire to join a fraternity while in college. However, attending various information sessions about multiple brotherhoods revealed a common interest they all shared: networking. Each organization always mentioned that there would always be frat brothers waiting to welcome me anywhere in the world. If there was anything I found admirable about fraternities, this was it. We all have different paths in life. Some people will be led to college while others will not. It's not necessary to be a member of a nationally recognized organization to share enduring friendships. When you meet people who are in line with your goals and beliefs, you'll naturally organize.

Choose friends who ask more of you than you ask of yourself. If you had a workout partner at the gym, would you want them to allow you to give up every time you felt defeated? I would hope not. The only way you're going to get your body into shape is by getting over your current physical and mental conditions. The great abdominal muscles we see in fitness commercials aren't made overnight. They are made with hard work, motivation, consistency, and in most cases, friends who push them to strive harder. Suppose your fitness partner was ready to quit after the first five minutes of arriving in the gym. What good are they going to be in the long-run success of your physical fitness? What good would you be to them if you did the same? What if you hired a personal trainer and they quit on you? Mentally, you would have to accept tackling your obstacles alone. The correlation between working out and the lives we live outside the gym should be apparent. Working on anything consistently should show progress in measurable terms. You should see the same progression from the various circles you associate with.

Are your friends encouraging you in the marketplace? It doesn't have to be every day, but we should all take the time to ask our friends how things are coming along with their goals. After listening to their response, offer them genuine feedback and encouragement. If you aren't already doing this, it's not too late. Showing interest in the aspirations of others is mutually beneficial. Never underestimate the power of speaking greatness into someone's life. The journey to success is challenging for most. The positive energy that we receive from our friends is like rocket fuel along a long stretch of unforgiving highway. We can possess a full tank of vigor, but many will be empty before reaching their goals. Getting too close to "E" can be extremely dangerous. This results in time-consuming holds on our objectives if we allow ourselves and those in our inner circle to get stranded on the highway of life. It's essential to remain consistent in your friend's life and vice-versa so that neither party is on the verge of becoming burnt out. Be supportive like a pitstop that refuels the ambitions of those around you.

Befriending People of Power and Influence:
Some of the most affluent careers in our country are secured by social connections. In today's world, this is known as social currency. Associating with a power player in an important industry has countless benefits. These can come from things like high-power references on platforms such as LinkedIn or an entry into a highly competitive industry. The marketplace has become so fierce that bachelor's degrees have become the new high school diploma. Value your connections.

Growing up, I watched kids migrate to those who were the most popular, beautiful, or best dressed. I used to always think to myself, "Why does everyone love that person so much?" Beautiful females seemed to only hang out with other girls who were equally attractive. Just as the girls did it, guys became male groupies to star athletes because they knew it would lead them to more girls. I never agreed with these types of friendships because they were based on selfish gains and leeching. There's a way to associate yourself with someone performing at a higher level without using them. That's by allowing them to teach and inspire you.

I'll never forget many years ago in Columbus, Ohio, I was refueling at a Speedway gas station when I saw an African American man stepping out of a Mercedes-Benz SL500 with a wool three-quarter coat, nice business suit, and polished shoes. This guy dressed for success and emitted an aura of confidence. We will call him Don. I was in my early twenties at the time when I approached him and asked, "Hey man, if you don't mind....what exactly do you do for a living?"

"I invest in real estate," Don replied.

At that moment, I never became so proud to see someone who looked like me that was doing something so positive in the world (considering the neighborhood I grew up in). From the looks of it, this guy was doing well. It gave me the kind of hope that endures for a long time. We eventually exchanged contact information so that we could meet again someday to discuss business. Later, I learned that Don had rental properties that numbered into the twenties with no intent to sell. He was building a residual monthly income that would allow him to spend the least amount of time working while earning passive income around the clock. I was the student, and Don was the teacher. I wasn't there to scheme on what I could take, but rather what I could learn. I was willing to work for free to learn the game. I gained much-needed information that he willfully gave. This was a priceless experience for me, considering that people are willing to pay real estate gurus thousands of dollars to have personal one-on-one access. I was getting mine free of charge because I introduced myself to someone performing at a higher level. At the time, it was hard for me to see twenty feet in front of my current situation, but he encouraged me to do more. Once I began to put more into my actions, I began to see my dreams unfold. Don has genuinely changed my life since that day at the gas station. Several years later, I formed a real estate company with family and began performing several real estate acquisitions all around central Ohio. I was slightly disheartened that Don never had the chance to witness the growth of the seed he planted. Unfortunately, we fell out of touch when he moved away. However, I'm still forever grateful and appreciative.

Be A Good Friend
Most teens grow tired of waiting to get their first vehicle and driver's license. When I was 15 years old, I immediately signed up for driving school. Upon completing my driver's

education, I started saving for my first car while working a summer job. My first vehicle was a 1988 Buick Skylark Custom. The vehicle was the color maroon inside and out. It was exciting to finally have the freedom to move around. It was fantastic having my own vehicle but being the only one among my friends was not. Many years after we had graduated from high school, my best friend still didn't have a car. I knew that he loved BMWs. We were much older and did many things that required driving, like going to work or going out on weekends. I would provoke him religiously, making comments like:

"Listen, man, it's pointless for you to always have to give people gas money to take you places when you could finance a car with low monthly payments. Besides, you can't continue being the best-dressed person at the bus stop! That's not cool! What will the girls think when you tell them to pick you up for dates!?" I would say.

Thomas and I joked very harshly toward one another because we were best friends. It was all funny but sadly true. After a bit of clowning around, I got serious. I began searching for vehicles that my friend could immediately purchase. After many disappointing attempts, I finally found a 1987 BMW 3 series that my mentor just so happened to be selling for $500. My best friend always wanted a BMW, so this was right on the money! Needless to say, he bought the car, and it lasted him quite a while.

Take a genuine interest in helping your friends find a resolution to some of their most challenging problems. Although we were much younger back then, I believe my teasing combined with a solution really pushed my friend into getting his first set of wheels. I knew I could playfully inspire him into getting a car, but I wouldn't suggest everyone else go about it that way. Know who you're dealing with before you give your advice. Depending on the person and the relationship you have with them, things might need to be approached uniquely. When offering your advice to others, remember that everyone will not be open to hearing your opinions.

Some people know how to take good advice and convert it into motivation, while sadly, countless people do not. One of the most challenging things I had to learn when dealing with family, friends, and associates was that everyone didn't want my advice. As ambitious individuals, we sometimes can be strongly opinionated. Only when asked, should you give your thoughts and opinions about their particular situation. It's easy to assume that people in your circle are willing to listen based on your relationship. However, sometimes, the other person just wants you to listen while they vent. Everyone moves at their own pace. What motivates you doesn't always motivate someone else.

Just as you enjoy others celebrating your victories, remember to always celebrate theirs. The inspiration friends receive from one another should be limitless and unconditional. Be an inspiration to all those you socialize with. Make sure to increase the time you spend with friends who uplift your spirit. Strategize and plan with your colleagues. Aspire to perform as those achieving at a higher level.

Seeds to Sow:
- It's widespread for people to love and support you if it doesn't appear you're getting ahead of their expectations.

- Team up with individuals who have like-minded objectives and discover all the positive benefits of working towards common goals.
- Spend more time lending your ear to someone who will keep you thinking. Be consistent and sharpen each other's minds regularly.
- Don't be afraid to introduce yourself to influential people. You just might get a much-needed break and befriend someone who may open several doors of opportunity.
- Muster the courage to discontinue or significantly limit relationships with friends who voluntarily choose to remain stagnant.
- Never resent another person's accomplishments. Perceive them as doors of opportunity left wide open.

The Fifth Seed
Environment Selection

Growing up in Cincinnati, Ohio, I went to schools that had paint falling off the walls, textbooks that were tearing apart, and a host of other outdated problems. One of the bad things about growing up in the inner city is that there is a lot of depression and discouragement because of the environment. I used to get so upset at my mother for not allowing me and my sister Nyiesha to go outside and play on the sidewalk with our friends. My resentment disappeared when I got older. Ghettos across America offer many negative influences and traps for the youth, and my mother knew this. Most children who were no older than six years old were already cursing like sailors. Every window had black bars on them like the local jails. Police were frequently on the scene arresting someone that you may have known. No one cared to keep the area clean and neat; trash was everywhere. This place was a real-life human "zoo." Like a horrible disease, children inherited the broken spirit of so many adults drained of their hopes and dreams. The Apostle at my church called this a "generational curse." Without the presence of ambitious people like you and I, children in run-down areas like the ones I grew up in are left with only drug dealers and athletes to look up to, and most of us never made it to the NFL or NBA.

Mom had an excellent plan. Although she may not realize what she had done for me while doing it, I will be forever thankful. My sister and I spent a lot of time at our grandparent's house because my mother knew that this environment was much safer. I also spent significant amounts of time with my father (whom I dearly miss). Silverton, Ohio, wasn't the

Hamptons of New York, but it was for a kid coming from downtown Cincinnati. In this area of town, you could see the difference in the environment and how it affected all those who lived there. Children were more optimistic, police were never present, and front doors could be left unlocked without the worry of a possible intrusion. There were fully manicured lawns present and not just patches of dirt and rock. The streets were clean, and you could hear the laughter of children playing outside year-round. It was a good community. You could almost smell the positive vibes that seemed to illuminate everything around you. Social communication was much different. Foul language constantly being heard in the city had transformed into very nurturing, kind words as strangers greeted you from their porches while passing through. This neighborhood was the best environment for my personal growth. Are you living in your Silverton? What will it take to get there?

My grandparent's house is where I first began my love for reading and genuinely discovering things. There were volumes of encyclopedia books to indulge in nestled in a wide bookshelf located at the top of the stairwell near the front door. I'd spend hours going through each book, letting my imagination run wild. It was the early nineties and having a small library of books such as these was undoubtedly not affordable at my residence. I believe Encyclopedia Britannica sets were going anywhere from $1,500 to $2,200 per set during this period! Grandpa and Grandma were clearly in a higher tax bracket! The practice of reading significantly increased my level of comprehension in other subject matters because many of them required that you read something to learn the underlying meaning. These were indeed pre-Wikipedia days and the convenience of high-speed internet!

Although today's high-speed global information network dwarfs what was available back then, I experienced the same benefits through reading. Another notable thing to mention is that being there provided me the gift of learning how to use and navigate a desktop computer. Can you see the advantage of my visits to my grandparent's home? Who would have ever known that technology would experience such exponential growth in such a short period? Spending time in that environment had rewarded me over and over through the years by the head-start it afforded me. Where would some people be today had they been given the same opportunity? Your surroundings matter because they usually (not always) will predict how you will spend your time when looking for something to do. The weekend environment at my grandparent's home also made me realize another observation. People were much happier in this neighborhood. If you grew up in a low-income community, as I did, you'd find many adults stressed to the max over financial struggles, local crime, etc. It's hard to find peace in a place where you're constantly worried about the safety of your children. Not having enough income to move your family away from such a hostile environment becomes even more discouraging. Thank God my mother had a plan. We eventually moved away from the wrong neighborhoods. I'm just grateful I had a positive place to nourish my educational and personal development, even if it was only for a weekend at a time.

Everyone who becomes a member of a golf country club isn't an enthusiast of the sport. Country clubs are usually breeding grounds for countless business deals that take place every day. I'm sure that there are some people out there swinging a nine-iron who have the slightest clue of what they're doing, but they see value in the networking experience that comes with an 18-hole game.

If golf isn't your game, you indeed shouldn't write it off. You will come to learn that sometimes you should go to potential opportunities to meet people you otherwise will never meet. Convenience is a luxury that you won't always have. You must be willing to effortlessly put yourself in places where you can gain a competitive advantage over the next person who's too lazy to do it. Ambition doesn't wait for an opportunity to fall in its lap. Sometimes creating a comfortable lifestyle for yourself will mean stepping outside of your comfort zone. Your next major break could be the difference in the places you choose to hang out. Have you ever visited a Starbucks or Panera Bread and taken a minute to observe what's happening around you? You will see people like yourself getting interviewed, working on laptops, signing documents, and many other business handlings simultaneously. How are the patrons dressed? What kinds of conversation can be heard over the chatter? Even if you're not there to meet someone, remember that environments such as this are contagious if you're looking for a place to get some work done. Choose environments that foster a high work ethic and allow you to meet others who are like-minded individuals.

Seeds to Sow:
- Never let your current circumstances dictate where you will spend your time. Find your place of peace so that you may flourish and develop.

- Be aware of the influential nature of the environments you give the most time.

- Widen the door of opportunity by discovering new business casual settings to meet people.

The Sixth Seed
Media Influence

Music

What does your favorite song mean to you? Why do you listen to it? Most of us have fallen in love and have songs that may bring us back to past relationships. I'm a firm believer that most people in the world enjoy listening to some form of music. Throughout history, music has been appreciated by the masses because it draws on your feelings. A collection of instruments has the power to summon emotions that can be good or bad depending on the correlation made between a previous, current, or future event.

People who find themselves in the gym religiously use their favorite songs to increase the intensity of their workouts. Without music, some people can't have an effective day while trying to get in shape. I want to focus on the music that inspires action. Can you think of a song or instrumental that causes you to "act" on your dreams? What songs can you think of that motivated you to do something without procrastination?

A significant part of the influence you receive will come from the things you allow yourself to hear. Be careful not to listen to music that will cause you to slow down on progressive activities. For instance, I don't listen to rhythm and blues while generating business for my company. Why? It may be different for you, but when I listen to R&B during my peak performance hours, it slows me down. I'll find myself not thinking about business but maybe about my current relationship or possibly an ex-girlfriend. It probably wouldn't be a good idea to do this. Love

44

is a beautiful thing, but as the saying goes: it doesn't pay the bills! It would be best if you focused on maximizing your potential each day. After working an entire shift and my business phone has been powered off, it's okay to slow things down. Being carried away in my thoughts would be okay during this time. The truth is that I love rhythm & blues music, but it's toxic to my drive while trying to complete daily goals. Leave everything that isn't business-provoking at the door when you leave home in the morning. Take a chance on classical music while studying or performing your work duties. It's been known to provide a clear mind while you complete your tasks. If that's not enough, you can always check out different songs that only include the instrumentals. Just remember to choose music that puts you in a creative, action-taking mode.

Most people born before 1985 can remember Mike Tyson fighting for the world heavyweight championship title and defending it multiple times. Mike Tyson had an impeccable career while boxing and instilled fear in the majority of his competitors. I'll never forget watching "The Tyson Fights," as we called them. The fights were always in Las Vegas, usually at the MGM Grand Casino. The lights would dim, and the cameras would flash endlessly while the fans roared at the grand entrance of "Iron Mike" Tyson! Although I didn't think much about it back then, I realized that Mike always came out to the same kind of songs as an adult. He chose music that intimidated his opponents! He never chose a love song as his entrance theme into the ring. Someone in his training crew (including himself) knew that music could summon a specific state of mind that would prepare him for a grueling, brutal battle. The music he allowed his ears to absorb had to correlate with physically punishing someone in the boxing ring. Thus, so many physical trainers listen to hardcore music while conditioning their bodies. Although he was a fictional character, Rocky

Balboa is another excellent example. One of the classic scenes in the original Rocky movie was when he ran up the stairs to the Liberty Bell and extending his arms in a victory stance. At the same time, training has won the hearts of many athletes and physical trainers. If you're not sure about the song, I'm referring to the song written by Bill Conti called "Gonna Fly Now."

Many of us won't earn millions boxing in Las Vegas, but whenever you have new goals, play songs that will motivate you to be the best! Remember, take advantage of the mindset that the music's lyrics and rhythms will put you in. Think about the vibes that the music creates for you and others around you. Be intentional about what, where, when, and how you listen to all music.

Film
I will never forget the way I felt after seeing my first Bruce Lee film. I could feel the adrenaline pumping through my veins and a swelling sense of courage. Watching Bruce Lee dismantle each opponent that came to destroy him was inspiring. The energy he created on film that passed to the viewer was unmatched. I would always get up feeling as if I could take on five men in a brutal fight! I felt like a warrior! I was high on vigor. At the time, I was unaware that I was going through the power of influence via film. As we all know, this kind of media can be good or bad for you depending on what you allow yourself to absorb daily. Allowing yourself to become immersed in various types of cinema begins to reprogram your thoughts.

Why do you think networks call it television "programming?" It would be a good idea to look at your brain as a computer that downloads everything it hears and sees from the world around you (which we will call the

Internet). If you knew that certain things you could listen to or see would risk the chance of you downloading a malicious virus, would you pay them any attention? Of course not! No one has the desire to be controlled by outside forces, which is what a virus would do to you and your plans. In the movies, and what you see on television is influential whether you want to accept it or not. It's essential to focus more than half of your free time on things that will benefit your future. The majority of people widely allocate their time to music, the Internet, and television shows. According to USA Today, in conjunction with Nielsen Media Research, the average home has more televisions than people living in them. What does a fact like that tell you about Western culture?

I recently watched a television ad that showed a man watching a movie in one room. He paused it and then proceeded to another room in his home to press play. America has become addicted to television and film media. What kind of conclusions can be discovered from something like this? Do we always have to be entertained? Are we miserably bored with our lives? In the same news article by USA Today, Nielson explains that the average person watches four hours, thirty-five minutes of television daily. If you dedicated two hours of that time daily for one year, you would have spent seven-hundred thirty hours investing into your future! That's approximately thirty days of compounding self-development!

One of the primary keys to your success is learning how to convert mismanaged time into something beneficial. Instead of watching a reality show and giving away countless hours, allow yourself to become absorbed into accomplishing objectives. Here are some examples listed below of how some television programming can relate to your field of expertise:

Your Goal - Related Television or Film:
Real Estate - HGTV
Investing - CNBC
Historian - History Channel
Veterinarian - Animal Planet
Your Interests - (search YouTube)

Television and music are not the only things creating new wrinkles in our brains. Audiobooks and print have allowed the sharing of valuable knowledge through centuries and decades of human existence.

Books
By reading or listening to this book, you have already begun to understand the power of its meaningful content. The act of reading will give you an extensive vocabulary that will boost your communication skills when done regularly. I've never in my life met someone who enjoys reading and can't hold an intelligent conversation. If you're someone who dislikes sitting in one place to read for hours, audiobooks may be your solution.

Listening to audiobooks can be done conveniently on your commutes to work, school, or just while out casually shopping. I'll admit; reading before bed makes me sleepy, so audiobooks are a Godsend. Residents in cities like Chicago, Los Angeles, Houston, and Atlanta can easily spend two or more hours per day commuting. Two additional hours each day will give you an extra 60 hours of monthly productivity! Leveraging your time with education during your commute will nourish your personal development.

Think of each unique talent or characteristic about you as being a tiny seed. How often you water it will be a determining factor in its development. Want to become a better speaker? It's always been my theory that reading books will increase your vocabulary, thus articulating your thoughts more clearly. When you're reading or listening to audiobooks, which seed will you water? Like any other media form, the micro messages you receive from reading have the power to shape your perspective. Everything you receive from your book collection isn't always something you should learn to do or put into practice. Many times it may be a thorough explanation of things to avoid.

If you've ever engaged in something you knew very little about and suffered a loss, what would having known spared you? Many people who have gone before you already paid the price for things you're likely to encounter. Lessons from others can save you countless time, energy, and money. If you were offered ten years of experiences in a book for twenty dollars, would that be worth it? Absolutely. You only need to be willing to receive the message. Commit time to read each morning before you start your day and observe how it sets the tone for things to come.

Seeds to Sow:
- It is important to remember that media can program your mindset in favor of your goals or work against them by subconsciously embedding negative values.

- Behavior comes from mindset. Mindset influences behavior. Behavior pushes you further away from your goals or brings you closer to them.

- Nourish your mental growth by keeping good literature in circulation to help you to learn from the lessons between its' pages.

The Seventh Seed
Image

Personal Image

Your image will be weighed heavily on how the marketplace considers you for more significant opportunities. Dress like the person you want to become. Make your appearance match the level of respect you would like to receive. I'm a great fan of many musicians and have been amazed at their fanbase retention and growth over their respective careers. I have a growing concern with those who decide to mimic a celebrity in ways that will not benefit their real-world lives. I could name countless things that would require me to write a separate book; however, two specific things must be mentioned. Those two things are personal image and the image of your business. Let's start with a personal image first.

In today's generation, most people have tattoos. Years ago, only the "bad boys" had their arms, chest, and legs inked to cover every available area of skin on their bodies. The majority of people make decisions on tattoos while still in their early adult years. Most tattoos are irreversible without spending a fortune to have them removed. I have a few tattoos myself, but they are concealable. One of my greatest pet peeves is a facial tattoo. I have no intention of offending anyone reading this book with tattoos on their face, but let's intelligently review some of the facts. If you are a celebrity with tattoos, depending on the type of entertainment you provide, in most cases, it won't matter how many you get or where you put them. Having millions of dollars in the bank (with sound financial planning) is usually sufficient to prevent you from subjecting yourself to the average W2 wages most Americans face. Although many people become wealthy in the entertainment and fashion industries, several are discouraged from getting tattoos based on the particular image they are being paid to maintain. Looking back at more than a decade ago, Victoria's Secret Models have always been a great example. According to Forbes in 2009, those listed below were the top ten paid models:

1. Gisele Bündchen- $25 million
2. Heidi Klum - $16 million
3. Kate Moss - $9 million
4. Adriana Lima - $7.5 million
5. Doutzen Kroes - $6 million
6. Alessandra Ambrosio - $5.5 million
7. Natalia Vodianova - $5.5 million
8. Daria Werbowy - $4.5 Million
9. Miranda Kerr - $4 million
10. Carolyn Murphy - $3.5 million

Now that you've seen the income and the names attached to the above model celebrities, I challenge you to Google each and every last one of them and show me one that has a tattoo on their face. So many A-list actors/actresses refuse to cover their bodies with tattoos because it may disqualify them from roles in movies. Although producers could use makeup in film, sometimes they may not want to go through the lingering hours of trouble it takes hiring makeup artists to paint over tattoos before getting any work done. One of the main things I want readers to understand is that no one is obligated to employ your skills or expertise! The models listed above have obviously gained a respectable amount of wealth, yet they remain consistent and serious about their personal image! They're aware that their appearance can directly impact the income and endorsement contracts they're awarded. So why are there so many young people dismissing their future opportunities on permanent skin fixtures which can't be concealed? What if they change their mind about what they want to do for a living? What if their new interests require a certain level of professionalism? Will they fit in? We all play a grave role in our own self-destruction. Unless you've already fulfilled your life goals, don't limit your opportunities by getting tattoos in places you can't conceal. Although it's not right to prejudge people, that's something you're going to have to let go of if you want to be competitive in the business marketplace.

While tattoos may be the least of problems for some ambitious spirits, their choice of attire can equally hinder their progress towards set goals. Dressing for the role you want to be in is paramount. I understand millions of people in the world may have very odd appearances but may be geniuses in disguise. Although the person wearing the clothes may be an expert in dentistry, that doesn't mean that the world around them will be accepting. Unless you have already developed a rapport with someone, the attire they're wearing will signal whether you may or may not do business with them. Someone I don't know wearing a t-shirt that's baggy enough to fit three people, and army fatigue pants will not be administering local anesthetics for my root canal procedure. How would you feel if a cardiologist wore swim trunks and flip flops while performing surgery on one of your parents? There's nothing wrong with looking like you're going to the beach or wearing beach attire. Still, it's simply not appropriate for every situation! Trying to resist the appearance of any given profession that has been conditioned for hundreds of years is an absolute waste of time depending on the industry. If you want people to take you seriously, you must first get over your own opinions and begin to accept how you must present yourself to be better received by the marketplace.

Business Image
The assumption that appearance no longer matters when you're self-employed is a fallacy. Even when working for yourself, you will always be selling the image of your business and services to consumers. One of the worst questions a customer could ask walking into your establishment is: "Do you work here?" Why should anyone have to ask a stranger whose shopping in their establishment if they're an employee? Have you ever walked into a store and had to find a staff member to assist you? How did you feel later after finding out that the sales associates were walking around dressed in ordinary clothes blending in with the patrons? I would assume that most people who have ever gone shopping in their life have experienced this type of annoyance at least once.

Some of the world's most respected companies are known to create non-negotiable dress codes for their employees. Whenever visiting The Cheesecake Factory, I've never had to ask who's working because their staff is usually wearing all white and a dark-colored tie. Other notable companies such as MAC Cosmetics require their representatives to wear all black. You should always have a uniform look for those representing your company, aka the image of your business. Customers appreciate familiarity and are likely to disassociate from any brand that fails to offer consistency.

Marketing Your Brand
Leave no stone unturned when marketing the image of your company. Growing up, we used to catch bus rides to Florence, Kentucky, where my mother would buy clothes for my older sister and me. She was strict about our appearance and did not want us publicly tarnishing her reputation as a parent. We were in fact, indirectly marketing our quality of life to the world.

Now that I'm a father, I understand things more clearly. My sister and I were a representation of our home while in public. My mother knew that people would be quick to judge us unfairly had we looked shabby. This would also make her directly accountable. Your business should be no different. Every person you hire will represent you and your company when you're away. Studies have shown that humans prejudge things based on appearance in a matter of three seconds. It's no wonder that companies spend millions of dollars annually on marketing.

Most of us have seen billboard advertisements while traveling from point A to point B. Have you ever noticed that these ads aren't filled with too much information? These ads usually get straight to the point. The reason is that they know that they only have a few seconds to deliver a lasting impression. The purpose of billboard marketing is to get your attention while you're in motion. This kind of advertising is what I call "reminder marketing" because companies are constantly reminding you about the products and services they offer. When you need the said product/service, the idea is that you will think of that specific company. During a week, you may be exposed to hundreds of ads on your phone, television, subways, bus stops, etc. One advertisement is usually the collective effort of several marketing professionals. Their job is to develop strategies to deliver a successful visual campaign in a short amount of time. What would your audience learn from only a few seconds of engaging with your marketing? How could you maximize the potential of such a short lease on their attention? Remember that the world is watching, and first impressions are everything.

Best Foot Forward
It isn't wise to be cheap when investing in your image. If you decide to take the less expensive route when presenting your business, people will notice. I will never forget the day I had a business meeting with a guy who ran a profitable company and was wearing one of the worst uniforms I had ever seen. I'll give him more credit than someone who wasn't trying at all. This guy probably went to a crafts store, printed his logo, and ironed it on his t-shirt. It was an excellent design, but it was not balanced. You could see the dark lines of a perfect square going around it from the transfer paper used to create it. Everyone doesn't know how to design, embroider, or print images to uniforms, so it would be wise to hire a professional.

Avoid wasting money and time having to go back and fix things that could have been executed correctly. Don't fall into the instant gratification trap by trying to build your image too fast. Strategize and develop at your own pace so that when you are ready to present your company to the world, it will appear as if you've been operating for years! It may not seem fair at times to spend the extra amount of money needed to attain a particular look, but it will be well worth it in the end. It's a known fact that people gravitate towards those who look great at what they do! Constantly remind yourself that your image while doing business isn't personal; it's business!

Instantly improve the image of your business with the following:
- professional website
- business cards
- customer reviews
- custom letterheads
- social media presence

- logos & trademarks
- registering your business with qualifying third-party companies
- office/store locations

Seeds to Sow:
- Court the attention your business receives with care. You may only get one chance to leave a lasting impression.

- Your image is paramount and must accurately reflect your values as an individual and company.

The Eighth Seed
Removing Fear

Bad Job; Great Experience

One of the worst jobs I've ever had in my life was the absolute best experience for developing my sales skills. I know this may sound confusing, so allow me to explain.

While attending The Ohio State University, I was the typical college student with an overdrawn bank account in need of any income I could muster. I saw an ad in the paper that promised I'd make a minimum of four-hundred dollars weekly, and it lured me like a fish on a hook. Surprisingly enough, when I got there, I found out that it was a one-hundred percent commissioned job and that I would be making door-to-door sales. I had experience from a clothing store in Cincinnati, Ohio, named Uptown Gear. There was a significant difference in experience working both places. At Uptown Gear, we were located in a brick-and-mortar establishment where customers could walk in and browse our selection. The new company in Worthington, Ohio was located in a business park not open to the public. This was when I discovered that we'd be selling random items like fountains and crayon sets door-to-door. When I worked at Uptown Gear, selling was easier for a few reasons:

1. The customers came to us
2. I personally liked the products
3. I was comfortable in an environment of hip-hop clothing and mixtape sales.

Working at my "bad job" robbed me of all the things that made me comfortable.

I had to go to my customers. We were instructed to walk into businesses and sell the products we had in our duffel bags. I can remember walking miles in the smoldering summer heat while adhering to our dress code: a shirt, tie, casual shoes, and slacks.

I didn't like any of the things we sold. We had everything from cheap game sets to faulty umbrellas. My non-endorsement of what I was selling was killing my sales pitch. I had to learn what it meant to be excited about selling a product externally while reserving my personal opinions.

I was not in my comfort zone. This was the first time in my life that my paycheck was going to reflect my diligence to win. There was no payment for slacking. Wasting time would only leave me deeper in debt. I remember one time I was out all day from 7 am to 7 pm and had only made forty dollars. I was livid!

As much as I hated working at this place, there were fundamental principles that I adopted that would help me run the businesses I operate today. I no longer hesitate to make a pitch to someone or introduce myself. If someone isn't interested in what I have to offer, I simply move on to the next person. I no longer waste time wondering why this or that person wasn't interested. I'm now willing to get through as many "no's" as I need to get to a solid "yes."

Getting dismissed as I walked into a store before I could say "hello" was mind-blowing. I'll admit, the first time I received a tongue lashing by a store owner was very hurtful. I wanted to give up and quit. I didn't like the idea of people belittling my job and being cursed out. I can recall so many people telling me to get a "real job." In this world, we are constantly selling ourselves. We sell our ideas daily. If the small things cause us to surrender to defeat, what will we do when things get ugly? Fear of receiving the same treatment from the next business owner slowed me down. Everything improved when I learned to let go of being afraid.

A very commendable individual is Tyler Perry. He went from being abused as a child and homeless as an adult, to becoming one of the wealthiest producers in Hollywood. Even amid having no running water and a place to sleep, Tyler Perry chose to pursue his dreams in film and stage plays! If fearlessness could be measured and extracted for sale, Mr. Perry would make a fortune selling his! It takes a special individual to stay positive on the inside while experiencing so much negativity from the outside world.

Fear is one of the most debilitating diseases to success you can possibly have. Fear is what stops people from believing in themselves. Fear puts everything in your life on hold. Can you imagine the type of inventions or contributions to the world fear has ruined? Fear is not welcome in the house of success. It is a handicap that will prevent you from reaching your maximum potential. Living with fear is like playing baseball with a blindfold, hoping to score a home run. You might get lucky every now and then, but if you want to score consistently, you'll need to conquer fear.

I love Nike's slogan, "Just Do It." Really, it's that simple. I'm sure most adults can remember their first crush in their early school days. Since guys typically ask women out, this feeling of fear is much more common among males. Me and my friends disliked when our crush would hang in a group of females. Some girls were so popular, they were rarely found in a solo setting. We all wanted them to be alone to avoid rejection with an audience. Fear is why men are still experiencing this in their adulthood. Most men in the world can admit to the guilt felt for not introducing themselves to a particular woman. Being a man myself, I understand how scary this can be. I've run across women that made my heart skip beats just being in their presence.

One distinctive way in which I know I'm too shy to introduce myself to a beautiful woman is when my muscles feel weak and rubbery, and my speech is nearly cut off. That's intense! As I became older, what "could have been" was not satisfying for me. I began to let go of fear and things improved by leaps and bounds in my dating life. There's a possibility that fear caused me to pass up a future wife. Who knows? Those are terms I can no longer live with. We all have our own version and perspective of success. However, when we judge where we are, in relevance to where we'd like to go, it can be intimidating like a woman's beauty. How are our desires able to weaken us with fear? Everyone wants to be happy, but most people are afraid of failure. You cannot fear failure while in pursuit of success.

How many business ideas have you honestly thought of, started, and then quit because you feared it would not work? The victory lap in a race is the most important, simply because most people break down during this time. After running eleven-hundred meters around a track, the last one-hundred meters will make or break most people. Many people find it easy to get fired up to do something, but only a few ever complete the set goal or task. Have you ever wondered why the crowd begins to stand on their heels as runners get to the final lap in a race? Everyone has become aware that the last one-hundred meters will filter the losers from the winners.

Sports gives the world remarkable analogies to the business world. Take the National Basketball Association, for example. The last three minutes of any basketball game literally becomes the longest part of the game in most cases. Why is this so? Coaches and teammates all know that every play must be mastered and timed efficiently to win the desired results. The entire game may have been played in a very mellow fashion, but the heat must be turned on during the final moments to secure a victory. During the NBA playoffs of 2011, the Miami Heat had every opportunity to win the game against the Dallas Mavericks. When the game had become truly serious in the fourth quarter, Dallas always managed to make a comeback and win against the Miami Heat! They would regularly emerge from a five or ten-point deficit when it counted.

Imagine the luxuries our modern civilization enjoys daily, such as the computer I'm typing on right now. Could you imagine your life without the Internet, cell phone, automobile, etc.? These things mentioned were ideas before they ever materialized into something we couldn't see ourselves living without. If you could travel back in time and stand next to the person that invented the cell phone and observed him giving up on his invention, what would you say!? Would you give him words of encouragement? You would probably say, "You've got to be crazy to give up on this idea! The world is going to change with your invention!" The truth of the matter is that people can't see into the future. If they knew the result, most people would not be afraid to pursue their dreams with blind faith. As humans, we make majority of decisions based on "proven" results. That's why being fearless is paramount. There are no guarantees when you decide to start a business if it's going to be successful or not. You can't be afraid of the unknown. A bird will never fly if it's too scared to spread its wings and take a leap of faith! Even when you fail, you still win from the lesson it provides!

Experience is the best teacher. Before Michael Jordan got his first NBA championship ring, he had to go through the growing pains of becoming a better athlete. Michael Jordan's reaction after winning his first NBA championship on June 12th, 1991 was heartfelt. You could sense the intense connection he had with basketball as he held the trophy close with emotion. Championship titles in sports are the results of the blood, sweat, and tears of those who have committed their lives for one victorious moment. It takes hard work to be the best, and being the best doesn't always mean that you will win each time. There are always lessons in between. Don't be afraid to keep trying. Resolve to let go of fear in all areas of your life and begin pursuing.

Seeds to Sow:
- If allowed, fear will prevent you from living life at your fullest potential.
- The fear of failure is being afraid of learning "what needs to be done to succeed."
- All success stories are valuable lessons, "gifts wrapped in failure."

The Ninth Seed
Financial Intelligence

Usually, when people begin to enjoy what they do for a living, they start making loads of money. What good does it do to make large sums of cash and have zero financial intelligence? Before beginning this chapter, I would like to send a special thank you to Robert T. Kiyosaki for giving me great perspective with his book "Rich Dad, Poor Dad." Mr. Kiyosaki is a blessing to those willing to learn a lot about real estate and financial intelligence! It would help if you remembered to change the way you think about money. Know the difference between an asset and a liability. Assets put money in your account while liabilities debit it! If you cannot grasp how to maneuver financially in the business world, success will be hard to sustain.

Many of us have played video games. Whenever someone plays a new game, wins become challenging to obtain. However, if you dedicated yourself to consistent practice, you would start seeing noticeable improvements to your gameplay. Another great thing about mastering a game is that you begin to know why other people aren't winning. You can then pinpoint the reasons for their poor performance and leverage their experiences to make better decisions. Financial intelligence can also be viewed as a game, and learning it has the power to end disparity and begin prosperity.

Blowing It
Sadly, many people have never experienced what it's like to have supreme purchasing power. What I mean by this is the feeling you get when you go to the best mall in your city or

town and come to the realization that there isn't anything on sale that you can't afford. What would you do with that kind of purchasing power? Too much money all at once can develop too much confidence for some individuals, resulting in self-destruction. I've seen it happen to people around me, and I've also been guilty of it myself: "The feeling of arrival." People who lack financial intelligence are usually only concerned with spending money to appear rich without truly possessing real wealth.

As an African-American, I come from a culture where people are admired for how much money they've spent on material possessions. Overindulgence is a habit that will only hurt you. Instead of accumulating real wealth, too many people in the world are only concerned with looking like they have money. The humor behind this is that millionaires usually want to keep a low profile. As the saying goes, usually more money leads to more problems. The road to success can be very wary, and many of us fall victim to instant gratification when given the opportunity.

The minute you feel tempted to gratify your financial gains, you will become your own roadblock. Money received as a death beneficiary isn't a great feeling for most personalities. For most people, a life insurance payout will be the most incredible lump sum of money they'll ever receive at one time. Do you know of anyone who received a life insurance check and burned through the cash with nothing to show for it? Have you ever wondered why so many celebrities break down when things go wrong financially? No matter the dollar amount, bad money habits can deplete anyone's bank account. When you possess a small or large fortune, there's always someone with a plan to remove it from your hands.

We've all heard stories of lottery winners who ultimately wind up broke in a short period. They all became poor again because they never changed their style of thinking when it came to money. They got rich and allowed their old habits to rob themselves of financial freedom. Why does a person who has only received a few thousand dollars believe that they've somehow made it in life? The world will tempt you the minute the taste of success touches your lips. Lottery winners who went broke didn't have money problems; they had a lack of financial intelligence. This proves that more money doesn't always convert to growth. Here's an example:

Pete always wanted a Mercedes automobile at some point in his life. While Pete was working for low wages, he couldn't afford his dream car, so he opted for a Kia in the meantime. (Kia's are very respectable vehicles, and I'm simply referring to the cost comparison, not quality.)

Here's Pete's financial report card before he got promoted:

Net Income- $26,500/annually
Kia Car Payment- $2,400/annually
Automobile Ins.- $1,200/annually
Apartment Rent- $8,400/annually
Gen. Living Exp- $12,000/annually
Pete has a positive flow of cash at the end of the year of $2,500

Here's Pete's financial report card after he got promoted and acquired his dream Mercedes :

Net Income- $42,500/annually
Mercedes Pymt.- $9,600/annually ($800/mo.)
Automobile Ins.- $3,000/annually ($250/mo.)
Upscale Condo- $12,000/annually

Gen. Living Exp- $18,000/annually
Pete has a negative flow of cash at the end of the year of $100

   Notice that Pete is barely making ends meet in the example given above after investing in liabilities to show off his newfound income. One of the most notorious mistakes people make when inheriting a large sum of money is the immediate need to purchase a new automobile. The Mercedes cost Pete $7,200 more a year than the Kia. Some people fail to realize that many of the liabilities we become suckered into leads to buying more liabilities! Pete had a nice-looking Mercedes-Benz and felt the need to upgrade his living arrangements to compliment his new vehicle! The condo cost Pete $3,600 more annually than his previous apartment. Pete wasted over $10,800 on things to make himself appear richer to the world but ended up making less than previous years! What would happen if Pete got laid off from work? His diminishing cash flow wouldn't be enough to sustain his current lifestyle. Pete had learned to spend his additional earnings on liabilities. Income-producing assets would have paid for Pete's upgrades. Purchasing assets is like buying money with money.

Fundamentals of Money
These days, it's a high chance that the money sitting in your bank isn't worth the paper it's printed on. America has long suffered the effects of greed over common sense, and the poor and middle class are paying for it. Before there was any money in our society, people bartered for goods and services. Gold and silver were at the top of the food chain for trading. Historically, it has always been a highly valued commodity. One key element to the United States as a world leader was before 1971 when our currency had a gold backing. We had enough gold to pay off any debt for every dollar we had in circulation during this time. During the

Nixon administration, our country moved away from the gold standard, giving birth to "fiat currency" (also known as rubber checks). Why did Nixon support this? The United States was overspending on war (Vietnam) and other senseless investments. After the United States' bank statements went negative, those in power decided it was okay to begin printing money. Some people call this "robbing Peter to pay Paul." The United States was paying for old debt with counterfeit checks. This has been widely known as the Nixon Shock. This travesty was inherited by all future taxpayers.

Who's Pulling The Strings? You Or Someone Else?
I recently watched a CNBC story about people who had invested upwards of three hundred thousand into their 401Ks. Many of them saw their money disappear in waves during the 2000 dot com bubble crash. The 2008 housing crisis soon followed, and more fortunes were lost. When you don't control what's influencing your financial decisions, you'll lose every time. These people had never taken the time to learn the financial lessons needed to manage and protect their investments. The majority handed their futures over to a money manager and hoped for the best. America is unique because we're very liberated to have control over our own lives. Putting your hard-earned cash into the hands of a banker is like purchasing the contents of a box without knowing what's inside first. It's impossible to know everything in life, which is why you will always pay for things you don't know! Educate yourself on what you heavily invest in. Resolve to learning how to read stock charts, keep up with the news, choose stocks, gauge risk tolerance, investment goals, and more. Being informed will put you in control of your stock market picks or any other investments.

Dependency

Falling into a cycle of enablement will cause you to waste countless valuable years. Needing emergency funds or assistance from anyone outside of yourself is usually a clear indication that you need better financial management. Dependency hinders the will of an individual to transcend beyond their current situation. Without financial intelligence, many individuals who inherit millions usually fumble the legacy created by their parents. If all your basic needs are met (free food, free medical, free dental, subsidized housing & utilities), why would you possess any motivation? All help is not good. If someone is willing to bail you out of any situation, what will this do for your personal growth? How does this build wisdom and character? We all know someone who has never had to deal with their own problems. These people had safety nets to catch them from any fall. Those bailing you out are enablers, and although they may genuinely love you, they're hurting you. When their assistance is cut off, life's trials will expose those who have not learned to manage on their own. You can cheat tests in any learning institution, but only experience will carry you through in the real world.

Have you ever loaned someone money and knew that you weren't going to get it back? You probably felt that way because you knew their habits, or their situation had worsened. People who aren't focused and determined to make things happen aren't going to be reliable. You can't do the same thing over and over and expect different results.

If a person lacks the desire to do better for themselves, giving them money today won't change their future. That's why I decided to speak on the influences and personal changes you must go through before reaching this point in the book. Most people know who they can and can't rely on to repay borrowed debt. I personally never liked owing anyone unless it was good debt.

There Is A Such Thing As Good Debt
After reviewing liabilities and their relation to debt, now would be the perfect time to introduce good debt. Good debt pays for an asset that monetarily outperforms the underlying debt owed. An example of good debt is a low mortgage on a rental property that produces a positive cash flow after overhead costs. Here's an example of a positive cash flow:

Gross Income From Rent $1,000.00/mo
Monthly Payment On Loan $650.00/mo
Property Taxes $100.00/mo
Positive Cashflow of $250.00/mo.

I know that some of you are looking at this example and thinking, "How am I ever supposed to build wealth $250.00 at a time!?" You're not banking on the $250.00. You're banking on the financing. Let's say, after five years of successful payments, you decide to refinance. Depending on your equity position, refinancing with a lower interest rate will significantly decrease your mortgage payments. It may also provide you with capital to reinvest tax-free. One thing to remember is that your credit will determine your interest rates and overall payment on anything you finance for your business. Maintaining excellent credit is paramount in your ability to leverage. Once you begin to show a track record of repaying loans, banks will eagerly give you more funding. Five years later, you will have also raised your rents because of inflation, so the picture could now look something like this:

Gross Income From Rent $1,200.00/mo
Monthly Payment On Loan $550.00/mo

Property Taxes $150.00/mo
Positive Cashflow of +500.00/mo.

After viewing the example above, you have doubled your monthly cash flow to five hundred dollars. You may also have an extra few thousand sitting in your bank account to purchase a liability such as a car. If you wanted to buy a new vehicle, you could do so with the extra cash you made on the refinance and guess who's paying the bill? You're right! The tenant who pays rent is paying for your new car! Guess what else is so sweet about this deal? You don't pay taxes on your loans because they aren't considered income. Now imagine doing this with ten properties instead of one! I hope that it has become clear that you can successfully live on good debt if appropriately managed. If this same house is sold in the future, you will have to pay taxes on the money gained unless you continue this for the remainder of your life! I can't stress enough the financial education and mindset you must have to make things like this work. Many people earning large sums of money for the first time will lose themselves. Just like our government, they will start to spend more than what's available, and their whole lifestyle comes crashing down. Done correctly, one can live an amazing life leveraging debt with proper financial literacy.

College Education
The game has changed. Many years ago, going to college and getting a degree would be all you had to do to make a decent living for your family. Just like the government pumping fiat currency into our economy, the influx of college degrees has minimized their value in the modern job market. This is the same reason many people have chosen to return to school to attain additional credentials.

I have two significant problems with our school system.

1. Schools don't teach financial literacy.

Although it's possible to make an extraordinary life for yourself as a lawyer, doctor, etc., you're still obligated to return to work regularly. If you stop going to work, the income will stop coming in. Earning a respectable salary can position you well for investing in alternative assets like real estate. If you live modestly and invest in assets, you will soon find that you have enough cash flow to leave your profession for good if that's what you decide to do. If your passion in life is to treat people with cancer, my hat goes off to you! We need people like that in the world! Give yourself the luxury of free will. Having to do something and doing something by choice are two different feelings!

2. College degrees aren't worth what they used to be years ago.

With the exception of a few, most people's careers can be replaced by new talent or tech for less pay. For example, anesthesiologists aren't easy to replace. Just because you have a degree does not mean that someone is entitled to give you a job. Having a college education also doesn't mean you're going to be wealthy. You are fully responsible for your financial success. Being rich doesn't mean that you must go to college. Ambition and what you ultimately "do" make you wealthy. If someone gave you a new car, what good is the car to you if you can't operate it? You will have to be educated on various levels and have some training to enjoy what you have. You can't be the driving force behind your money by simply having a degree. Most people with degrees have jobs that make them passengers while the companies they work for are in the driver's seat. People who own businesses and know how to delegate responsibilities to others are in the driver's seat!

Assets Over Liabilities

What is an asset? An asset is something that creates income and is like the gears to cash flow. Investing in assets will consistently help you to build your income portfolio. One shoe doesn't fit all situations. An asset in one business may represent a liability in other businesses.

Here are a few examples of assets:

Work Vehicles: If you own a plumbing business, a utility truck will automatically become an asset because it allows you to make house calls to your customers. If you were a doctor, you wouldn't need to own a utility truck. You could travel on public transportation or purchase an inexpensive automobile. The truck wouldn't be an asset in your given situation but would be essential for plumbers.

Rental Properties: Having real estate is not an asset if it's not generating income for you. Unless your rental income can consistently surpass the cost of the mortgage, property taxes, insurance, maintenance, etc.; this will be very hard to achieve.

Pizza Oven: Owning a pizza parlor would not be complete without having a commercial-sized pizza oven that can bake several pizzas at once. The range would help to create the main product driving your business. In most cases, a commercial pizza oven in your residence would be a complete waste of money!

Income Types

Earned Income (also known as Active Income): If you receive a paycheck or salary from a company for the services you provide regularly, that's earned income. This is also known as *active* income. This means that unless you act, there is no income. The disadvantage of earned income is that you don't get tax write-offs for work-related expenses that could reduce your overall tax liability. Earned income is the highest taxed income by Uncle Sam.

Examples of Earned Income Careers:
- Retail Store Managers
- Dental Hygienists
- Police Officers
- Teachers
- College Professors
- Table Waitresses

Portfolio Income represents paper assets like stocks, bonds, certificates of deposit, hedge funds, etc. You invest in paper assets to receive dividends as a shareholder. This kind of income is taxed less than earned income depending on how long you hold the asset but doesn't offer any tax benefits.

Passive Income might only require you to spend a few hours weekly to check on its progress. Passive income does not require your presence for income generation; hence you will not be actively participating in the day-to-day business affairs.

Examples of Passive Income:
- Rental income from real estate investments
- Any business that you invest in as a silent partner

Of the three various forms of income listed above, the one that will offer you the most benefits will be passive income. I'm not telling you to quit your day job, but instead, begin developing a plan to purchase assets that will increase your net worth over time.

Although it's not the only route to take, real estate has always been a favored path to building wealth. After purchasing a residential property and making it livable, you will have gained an asset that can stay in your family for generations. Rental properties can be a blessing to your children accompanied by financial literacy. Remember, an asset is only profitable to the person who knows how to play the game! Without financial literacy, any asset in the world can become a worthless liability.

Seeds to Sow:
- Spend money to purchase more assets and not liabilities. Position your assets to pay your living expenses and liabilities and create generational wealth.
- Resolve to earn as much passive income as possible to decrease your dependency on others and your day job.
- Know the difference between good debt and bad debt.

Victory Lap (Closing)

As you approach your own victory lap in life, you can see the finish line in the near distance. Life's obstacles will have exhausted you after hurdling countless problems and unplanned events. This is the point in your journey where you will either win or lose. It's time to get your second wind and draw on energy that your body may not have, but your mind does. Now that you've re-calibrated your thoughts, begin to think about your personal wealth and overall self-development. Prepare to be met with adversity. I appreciate how the world speaks about how great life is once you've reached your goals, but no one ever talks about what comes with it. Remember to always stay focused! Two things will indeed happen when you begin to see success in the near distance:

1. Some people will only be happy for you as long as you haven't surpassed their expectations. If you aren't causing anyone to doubt you, you're probably not doing as much as your potential allows! You will have a clear understanding of the dedication and sacrifice it will take to get you where you're going, but naysayers won't. All they will see are your wins but be ignorant to the incredible journey you've endured.

2. Anyone that has ever created something that became a success has been mimicked. This is nothing to be upset about. Receive these gestures as a compliment! Have you ever noticed that whenever McDonald's opens a restaurant

on a corner, competitors like Burger King will immediately open across the street? Like Burger King and McDonald's, fast food giants spend millions of dollars on demographic research to strategically place their franchises to gain significant profits. You could assume that if one of these franchises opens a new restaurant, it would be safe for you to open your burger franchise across the street because they've already done the necessary homework! Walgreens and CVS pharmacies do this same kind of shameless competition. Everyone knows that McDonald's has been the world leader in selling burgers. After being the center of emulation for so many decades, one should ask the following:

How does a company like this stay ahead of fierce competition? When McDonald's Ray Kroc was asked the same question, his response was, "We can invent faster than they can copy." - Ray Kroc.

The keyword here is "invent." To ward off the competition, you will consistently need to reinvent yourself. All of history's "greats" will be imitated. Even our government knows this. That's why whenever you invent something in the United States, you will have to submit a patent for your idea so that you may be the only one to legally profit from your invention for a set period. After your patent expires, it will be a free-for-all for those who will make the knock-off version of your original idea.

Hearing things like "You've changed!" will be commonplace. People will despise your ideas because it wasn't theirs first. Your change will cause them to become uncomfortable with themselves, and they'll begin to reevaluate their own lives. I believe this is the same reason many people don't like acknowledging God because it makes them aware of self-accountability. Most people are comfortable if they can keep you in their rear-view mirror. To graduate from any level of sedentary behavior, one must heavily consider change. The anchor must be lifted from the water so you can sail towards a destination! The world is constantly changing, so keeping up is inevitable. It's possible that someday the principles in this book will become outdated, and we will all have to make yet another major shift to maintain a mediocre level of success. Think like Ray Kroc and enjoy reinventing your image, ideas, and total self!

In the end, it won't matter how many jobs you worked; but the careers you created. The degrees and accolades that adorn your walls won't matter either; rather, it will be the people you taught. The material possessions you collect will be insignificant; what you gave away will not. Every failure will eventually pass away, but the good seeds you sew will not. In the end, it won't be about how fast you made it to success, but rather the encouragement your story gives others. It won't be about all the friends you currently have, but rather those who will keep your legacy alive long after you've passed. Don't grow old and remorseful about what you could have done; instead, grow old with your accomplishments. Remember, a well-kept garden flourishes forever.

About the Author

"Dwayne Lattimore is a longtime founder of several start-ups, writing his first book Nine Seeds to Sow for Personal Growth at age 33 and completing it at 39. Now a full-time information technology professional, Mr. Lattimore and his children call the Atlanta area home. You can visit him online at www.thinkweconomy.com *or on Instagram (@think_weconomy)."*